They S
a Storm

Left to right: Sisters Norma and Barbara Webber push a floating white pine log with peaveys, while Mildred Sobel uses a pike pole to guide the log to the sawmill's ramp. All three are dressed alike and wearing L.L. Bean Maine Hunting Shoes. *(AP Photo)*

They Sawed Up a Storm

The Women's Sawmill at Turkey Pond, New Hampshire, 1942

By Sarah Shea Smith

Published by Jetty House
An imprint of Peter E. Randall Publisher
Portsmouth, NH

Copyright © 2010 Sarah Shea Smith
All rights reserved.

Published by Jetty House
An imprint of Peter E. Randall Publisher
Box 4726, Portsmouth, NH 03802-4726
www.perpublisher.com

(ISBN 13) 978-0-9828236-2-0
(ISBN 10) 0-9828236-2-2

Library of Congress Control Number: 2010938697

For additional copies, go to:
    www.turkeypond.com

or write to:
    Sarah Smith
    31 Smith Garrison Rd.
    Newmarket, NH 03857

Book cover, page design, and composition by Ed Stevens Design
www.edstevensdesign.com

Contents

Acknowledgments iii

Preface iv

1. The Great Hurricane of 1938 1

2. A Hurricane Forms 5

3. Timber-Salvage Operations 13

4. The Sawmills at Turkey Pond 25

5. The Women's Sawmill at Turkey Pond 31

Selected References 55

About the Author 59

Acknowledgments

Some of this text first appeared in the magazines *Northern Woodlands* and *The Northern Logger*. I would like to thank all of my colleagues who encouraged me to pursue the story. Special thanks to John Willey, for introducing me to the women at Turkey Pond; the Durant family, for sharing their story; the University of New Hampshire Cooperative Extension, for allowing me the time to research the story; all of those who graciously permitted me to interview them; Linda Wilson and Jim Garvin, at the New Hampshire Division of Historical Resources, for their enthusiasm and encouragement; Peg Boyles, for her gentle prodding; Debbie Anderson, for her technical skills; and my husband, Peter Smith, and niece Lauren Shea for lugging AV equipment and listening to my presentation way too many times. I would also like to thank Steve Long, of *Northern Woodlands* magazine, and Eric Johnson, of *Northern Logger* magazine, for helping me get the word out about this story.

Preface

Old sawdust seems to last forever. The old sawdust appearing like sand on the shore of Turkey Pond in Concord, New Hampshire, is the result of a series of events that began more than seventy years ago with the great hurricane of 1938 and ended with a group of women operating a sawmill at the pond during World War II.

I first learned about the women's mill at Turkey Pond from John Willey, the son of one of the women who worked there. John, who was operating a sawmill in Andover, New Hampshire, at the time,

Violet Story lifts a board to the edger operated by Barbara Webber. (right), Barbara guides the board through the edger, which squares its sides. *(Photos by John Collier Jr., Library of Congress, Prints & Photographs Division, FSA/OWI Collection, LC-USW3-034163 and 034130)*

shared his mother's scrapbook with me—a tattered collection of snapshots and newspaper clippings depicting the women at work between 1942 and 1944. Laura Willey and about a dozen other New Hampshire women were employees of the Turkey Pond #2 sawmill, built by the U.S. Forest Service's Northeast Timber Salvage Program in 1942 to saw hurricane-salvaged logs still floating in Turkey Pond four years after the historic storm.

Although my story focuses on the women at Turkey Pond, their story takes place during a period of time that shaped the history and landscape of New Hampshire—the 1938 hurricane and America's entry into World War II.

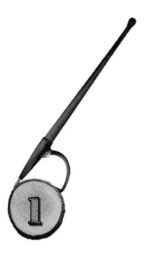

The Great Hurricane of 1938

Talk to anyone of a certain age and he will describe as if it were yesterday where he was when the 1938 hurricane hit. New Hampshire forester Roger Leighton was a sophomore forestry student at the University of New Hampshire in 1938. When the hurricane stormed in, he was at Nesmith Hall on the campus in Durham.

"It had been raining all week," Leighton recalls. "When I went to go home, I could see that most of College Woods was gone." College Woods, a fifty-five-acre stand of spectacular white pines adjacent to the campus, was badly damaged. Yet it represented only a fraction of the 2.6 billion board feet of timber that was felled by the great storm.

Ralph Page, who was a country dance caller from Keene, New Hampshire, described the storm:

> The hurricane pounced on us as quickly as that. Our house shook from the wind as if a mighty Paul Bunyan was leaning against it. My first inkling that it was anything different came when part our living room windows broke with a crash. A chair had been put

against the front door knob to hold it shut. Suddenly, the door was blown open. The wind had a fearful whine and crying sound, almost continuous, varying in intensity, and every few seconds stronger puffs would come. It eased off a bit in strength after an hour and a half but did not die out a great deal in strength or sound until shortly after midnight.

Old Lowell Road, in Nashua, is barely passable. *(From* Freak Winds, *by permission of Cummings Printing, Manchester, N.H.)*

The hurricane of September 21, 1938, was one of the most destructive natural disasters ever to hit New England. More than six hundred people died, most drowned in the storm surge that inundated coastal areas of southern New England. Property loss exceeded $400 million—equivalent to $5.5 billion in today's dollars. Winds in excess of a hundred miles per hour blew across the landscape; houses and barns were ripped apart. Collapsing barns crushed thousands of cows and millions of chickens. There was little people could do to prepare; there just wasn't enough warning. Nor could they have imagined the destruction the storm would bring.

High winds cause the roof to blow off the Silbulkin Shoe Company in Manchester. *(From* Freak Winds, *by permission of Cummings Printing, Manchester, N.H.)*

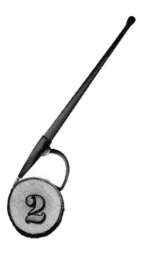

A Hurricane Forms

The storm (storms were not named until the 1950s) began as a tropical depression off the west coast of Africa. Today, meteorologists have satellite imagery and sophisticated communication systems to forecast and track storms. In 1938, weather forecasters relied on first hand accounts of storm activity, which was then radioed ahead to unsuspecting communities.

It should come as no surprise, then, that the first reports of the 1938 storm were received from a ship at sea. On September 16, the SS *Alegrete*, a cargo ship (later torpedoed during WWII), sailed into the storm off the coast of Puerto Rico and radioed the weather bureau in Florida that it was experiencing hurricane-force winds.

The U.S. Weather Bureau issued hurricane warnings for the Florida coast on September 19. Forecasters fully expected the hurricane to come ashore in Florida, where citizens were already preparing for the worst. At the last moment, the storm veered to the north and continued to move up the East Coast, passing Cape Hatteras, North Carolina, and

Virginia Beach. At midnight on September 20, the Cunard liner *Carinthia* (also torpedoed during the war) recorded a barometric pressure of 27.85 inches, which compared with a calm-weather reading of 30 inches indicated stormy weather along the Virginia coast.

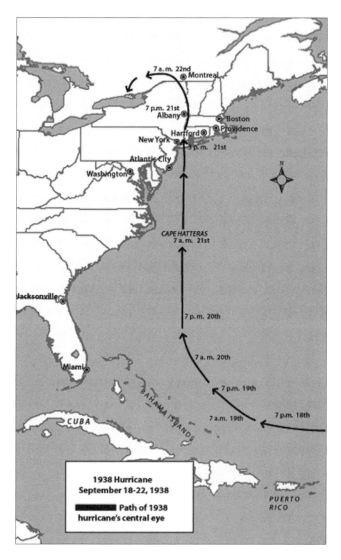

The unnamed hurricane moved crossed the Atlantic toward Florida but made a last-minute turn to the north. Notice how quickly the storm moved from Cape Hatteras, North Carolina to Long Island, New York. *(NOAA Coastal Services Center)*

By one o'clock in the afternoon on September 21, the weather bureau was overwhelmed by reports from ships in the vicinity, placing the storm one hundred miles east-southeast of Atlantic City, New Jersey, moving at seventy miles per hour. At three o'clock that afternoon, the bureau issued storm warnings for Long Island and Connecticut.

Unfortunately, the fast-moving hurricane, by then a Category 3 storm with winds approaching 130 miles an hour, had already made landfall, washing across Long Island and smashing into the southern New England coast.

Providence, Rhode Island, was particularly vulnerable because of its location at the northern tip of Narragansett Bay—a giant funnel. The storm surge, driven by the wind and tide, submerged the city. The sea continued to rise along the waterfront and by five o'clock. Providence was covered with ten feet of water.

In her book *Sudden Sea*, R. A. Scotti describes the submerged city: "The bay washed over Providence, six feet, ten, twelve, over roofs of cars, over the tops of trolleys—fifteen, seventeen feet—inundating three miles of industrial waterfront and the one-mile-square business district."

Helen Joy Lee, of Watch Hill, Rhode Island, describes her survival in Minsinger's *The 1938 Hurricane*: "I saw our 3-car garage lift up and dropped into the bay," she said. "I had to hold on with both hands against the force of the wind. I got soaked with each wave as it went over the house."

Later, as Helen fought for her life, she said: "Pieces of wood, shutters, doors, and chairs were flying through the air. Some were hitting me. I saw a small porch roof, perhaps my own, right-side-up, so I pushed through wreckage for about ten feet and got on the leeward side and climbed up. I just settled when a wave capsized it and I went under."

Helen Joy Lee survived the great storm but many others did not, drowned in their own homes.

Cities and towns farther inland suffered as well. Rivers, already at flood stage from the torrential rains that fell throughout September, spilled their banks. Hartford, Connecticut, received fourteen inches of rain for the month and Keene more than ten inches. Bridges were swept away, roads collapsed, and dams let go. In addition to devastating floods, Peterborough, New Hampshire, suffered a massive downtown fire that destroyed much of the central business district.

Fire, floods, and wind devastated downtown Peterborough. *(From* Freak Winds, *by permission of Cummings Printing, Manchester, N.H.)*

What the water didn't get the wind did. *The 1938 Hurricane,* by William Elliott Minsinger, provides a sober look at the track of the storm using hourly weather data from September 16, when the storm was moving across the Atlantic, until September 22, when the weakened low moved north of Montreal.

Weather interpretations generally agree that the 1938 hurricane was large—more than two hundred miles in diameter—that the eye was approximately forty miles wide, and that the storm traveled across the center of Long Island and north through New England slightly west of the Connecticut River.

Fast-moving, the storm center passed over Long island at three o'clock on September 21, New Haven at four, and southwestern Massachusetts at five. Just before nine o'clock, the weakened storm reached Burlington, Vermont.

North Atlantic hurricanes rotate in a counterclockwise direction and, depending on their size, generate tremendous winds around the vortex. As a storm moves across the ocean, it picks up moisture and whips it ashore as torrential rain. Hurricanes generally lose strength and slow down as they drag across the landscape, as did the 1938 hurricane.

When the storm hit Long Island, it was moving forward at seventy miles an hour in a northerly direction with winds blowing sixty to eighty miles an hour. The combination of storm rotation and forward motion created sustained winds in excess of one hundred miles per hour on the east side of the vortex, where the wind direction was from the south.

The Blue Hill Observatory, in Milton, Massachusetts, recorded gusts in excess of 180 mph. Mount Washington, in New Hampshire, clocked the winds at 116 mph, with gusts exceeding 150 mph. Winds were stronger on the eastern side of the eye. Rains, spinning off the cyclone, were heavier west of the eye.

The summer of 1938 was one of the wettest in New England's history. By the time the storm hit, most rivers and streams had already spilled their banks and the ground was saturated. To make matters worse, record-breaking spring floods two years earlier, in 1936, had weakened bridges and undermined riverbanks, all contributing to the damage from the 1938 storm.

Concord suffered devastating floods. *(From* Freak Winds, *by permission of Cummings Printing, Manchester, N.H.)*

Topography and forest type were also contributing factors. As winds moved across the relatively flat, sandy sections of southern New Hampshire and eastern Massachusetts, large stands of white pine simply blew over, their shallow root systems giving way. In mountainous and hardwood regions, the damage was more irregular, as the wind funneled up valleys and slammed into ridgetops. Areas of the White Mountains suffered landslides caused by the torrential rains.

Many historic accounts describe the severity of the great hurricane of 1938 in terms of property damage. Numerous grand Victorian homes were swept into Long Island Sound, some with their occupants still inside. Church steeples broke off. Stately elm trees toppled and bridges collapsed. Along the coast, boats were driven onto the rocks by the fierce wind and storm surge.

Keene was hit hard by strong winds. Note the snapped-off church steeple, which penetrated the First Congregational Church. Below, Sargent Garage, on Mechanic Street loses its roof. (From Freak Winds, by permission of Cummings Printing, Manchester, N.H.)

Giant elms tipped over in front of the state capitol. (Photo courtesy of New Hampshire Division of Forests and Lands)

White pine trees snapped off in Rollins Park, Concord.
(Photo courtesy of New Hampshire Division of Forests and Lands)

In northern New England, the destruction of the forests was as catastrophic to local communities as was the structural damage in southern New England. The forest, which provided wood to the timber industry, served as the economic foundation for many rural towns. The 1938 hurricane destroyed fifteen million acres of New England forestland, representing 35 percent of the forested cover.

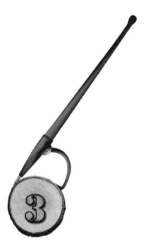

Timber Salvage Operations

As soon as the roads opened up and the immediate emergency needs were met, officials from each of the New England states began to assess damage to forests. Local foresters and others familiar with the timber resource assembled their best estimates of the volume of timber leveled or damaged by the huge storm (see table 1).

The New England State Foresters, the highest-ranking forestry officials, established the following priorities: fire prevention, hazard reduction, and timber salvage. In collaboration with the U.S. Forest Service, crews from the Civilian Conservation Corps (CCC) and the Works Progress Administration (WPA) who were already operating in the region immediately set to work to help reduce the fire hazard, first on federal lands and then on state and private lands.

An estimated 2.6 billion board feet of timber lay on the ground, an amount greater than today's annual sawmill production in Maine, New

Timber Salvage 1938 Hurricane
(volume is estimated in thousands of board feet)

State	Down Volume	U.S. Forest Service Salvage	Private Salvage	Total Salvage
Maine	50,000	48,187	68,840	118,027
New Hampshire	1,005,000	417,025	200,000	617,025
Vermont	360,000	65,781	30,000	95,781
Massachusetts	1,000,000	127,817	175,000	302,817
Rhode Island	85,000	11,814	18,000	29,814
Connecticut	150,000	19,759	67,055	86,814
Total	2,650,000	690,383	559,895	1,250,278

Table 1

Source: "Report of the US Forest Service Program Resulting from the New England Hurricane of September 21, 1938."

Hampshire, and Vermont combined. To compare, an average fifteen-hundred-square-foot house uses approximately fifteen thousand board feet of framing lumber. The storm blew down enough lumber to frame more than 170,000 homes.

Forestry officials were overwhelmed by the challenge of reducing the fire hazard and proceeding with a massive salvage effort. In a 1987 article in the Society for the Protection of New Hampshire Forests'

They Sawed Up a Storm 15

U.S. Forest Service employee Joseph Kaylor surveyed a spruce blowdown near Grantham. *(Photo: Bluford W. Muir, National Archives)*

Forest Notes, then-state forester Ted Natti wrote, "The fire hazard, usually moderate in New Hampshire, was in a critical state. Pine and other trees piled in twisted tangles would soon be highly flammable. Access roads were blocked and passage through the forest areas was virtually impossible."

New Hampshire officials looked to the forest industry to help devise a plan that would ensure that landowners would have the incentive to salvage wood. The plan also needed to protect lumber markets already weakened by the ongoing Depression.

The plan developed in New Hampshire became the timber-salvage plan for the entire region. On October 8, a mere seventeen days after the storm, President Franklin D. Roosevelt directed the U.S. Forest Service to assume leadership in the hurricane-ravaged area. The plan called for assistance from the federal government to coordinate and implement a massive salvage effort intended to recover and utilize the downed timber.

The program, called the Northeast Timber Salvage Administration (NETSA), was designed to create the incentive for private landowners to salvage timber by providing a market for the damaged logs. The U.S. government would provide the cash necessary to get the program moving. Even with federal funding, the salvage effort was daunting. Much of the timber was a tangled mess that proved dangerous for even the most experienced woodsmen. In 1938, crosscut saws and axes were still the most common tools used to harvest timber. The broken-off, uprooted, and mangled trees were processed by hand and moved by horse, mule, or oxen. Tractors were used in only a few instances.

The work was treacherous and time consuming. Sam Silver, of Boscawen, New Hampshire, was a young lad at the time of the hurricane and worked throughout the area logging on private land. He still recalls the piles of blown-down timber: "We used horses and crosscut saws. It was slow going," he says.

Horses pull a scoot-load of logs onto the ice at Lily Pond in Gilford. *(Photo: Bluford W. Muir, National Archives)*

No chain saws here! In 1938, most work was done with crosscut saw and ax. *(Photo: University of New Hampshire Cooperative Extension film strip, 1939)*

John Dunbar, also from Boscawen, was eighteen at the time and worked in many sawmills as a lumber stacker. He recalls, "The trees were tipped right over. They used horses and oxen and crosscuts and axes. It was all crisscrossed—the danger in it. But it helped the economy—it was a godsend. Gave everyone something to do to make some money. Money was scarce."

The U.S. Forest Service directed landowners to bring their wood to designated concentration areas, usually located at ponds or fields. After the wood was measured to determine volume, it was either dumped into a pond (or, in the winter, dragged onto the ice) or stored in fields. White pine and spruce, the more perishable species, were generally stored in the water. The water served to cool the logs, thus preventing stain and insect activity. The rest of the logs, hardwood and hemlock, were piled on land.

Unloading salvaged logs from ox-drawn scoot in Gilford on October 28, 1938. *(Photo: Bluford W. Muir, National Archives)*

Men use pike poles to corral floating logs. *(Photo: University of New Hampshire Cooperative Extension film strip, 1939)*

Eventually, 260 ponds and 675 fields throughout New England served as storage sites for hurricane-salvaged logs. The U.S. Forest Service leased the property from the owners, often at a dollar a year. By 1939, it held more than fifteen hundred leases across six states.

Landowners hired loggers or worked their own woodlots to salvage what they could. Logs were brought to the concentration sites, where a government scaler assessed volume and quality of the wood to determine price. Prices for logs averaged from twelve dollars per thousand board feet (MBF) for pine to twenty-four dollars for maple. After they were measured and tallied, the logs were branded with the U.S. Forest Service logo to confirm ownership.

A U.S. Forest Service scaler measures logs. *(Photo: University of New Hampshire Cooperative Extension film strip, 1939)*

U.S. Forest Service scaler brands logs with US logo to confirm ownership. *(Photo: Bluford W. Muir, National Archives)*

The Galford Lumber Company moved from Green Bank, West Virginia, to Northfield, Massachusetts. This picture was taken in February 1939 by Hayes Bigelow, of Brattleboro, Vermont. *(By permission from Patchwork Films, Lewisburg, West Virginia)*

U.S. Forest Service officials planned to sell logs back to the private market, enabling the sawmills to recoup costs. Unfortunately, as the salvage effort increased, not enough water storage was available to accommodate all of the softwood logs, and most local sawmills were already flush with wood and unwilling to pay the higher prices the U.S. Forest Service was asking. Faced with rapidly accumulating piles of wood, the U.S. Forest Service again looked to its private-industry partners for advice. By January 1939, a government sawmilling program was hatched.

The new program required the U.S. Forest Service to contract with private sawmillers to set up at the log-storage sites. The government contracted with the mills at a rate of $7.50 per MBF, which included sawing and stacking the lumber according to strict government standards. Jim Colby Sr., of Boscawen set up numerous sawmills, one in Rollins Park, Concord. While working at another, alongside The Bay in Salisbury during the winter of 1942, Jim fell into the icy water. "I was lucky to survive with all of those heavy clothes on. That was the first time I had rum," said Jim, referring to a home remedy for warming up.

Portable sawmills came from West Virginia, Wisconsin, Pennsylvania, and elsewhere to saw the salvaged logs. From the book about the film *Out of the Storm: The Galford Lumber Company Documentary Project*, B. J. Gudmundsson and Doug Chadwick tell the story of the move of one sawmill from West Virginia.

> By Christmas, just three weeks after the government announced the plan, Glen Galford, of Green Bank, West Virginia, made arrangements with New England Timber owner Frank Williams to salvage his fallen trees. Williams signed on a crew of more than thirty men, assembled the machinery and animals to do the job, and arranged for the whole shebang to get to New England in the dead of winter.

A team of horses skids logs to the Wilkens sawmill, near Chesterfield, on October 20, 1938. *(Photo: Bluford W. Muir, National Archives)*

Unknown sawyer processes hurricane-damaged logs. *(Photo: University of New Hampshire Cooperative Extension film strip, 1939)*

Workers stack white pine boards on stickers to ensure good drying. *(Photo: University of New Hampshire Cooperative Extension film strip, 1939)*

A government official inspects lumber piles. Note the overhangs, which shed water, and the straight and level piles, which ensure flat boards. *(Photo: University of New Hampshire Cooperative Extension film strip, 1939)*

After air drying, the lumber was sold to private lumber brokers. The largest sale was 425 million board feet of square-edged lumber, sold to the Eastern Pine Sales Corporation, a group of wholesale brokers, for twenty-one dollars per MBF. The Eastern Pine Sales Corporation, which sold lumber to a larger, regional market, facilitated the sawing and marketing of hurricane salvage timber. By and large the program worked smoothly, and by 1942, only forty-two sawmills were still operating under the NETSA sawmilling program. By 1943, the figure had dropped to less than a dozen.

After the attack on Pearl Harbor, on December 7, 1941, and our entry into World War II, much of the hurricane lumber was manufactured into ammunition boxes, crates, and other materials in support of the war effort. Some speculate that without the war, the lumber sawn as a result of the hurricane salvage effort may never have been completely used. Eventually, six hundred million board feet of timber was salvaged in New Hampshire, an amount equivalent to sixty thousand tractor-trailer loads of lumber.

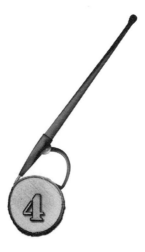

The Sawmills at Turkey Pond

Turkey Pond, on the west side of Concord, New Hampshire, was filled with twelve million board feet of white pine, the largest deposit of hurricane-salvaged logs anywhere. The shallow, gravel-bottomed pond was convenient and close to many of the largest blowdown areas. Due to the large volume of wood, the U.S. Forest Service had difficulty attracting a contract mill to set up on its shore. Finally, in June 1941, the first mill was brought to Turkey Pond, by H. S. Durant and family of Maine.

"We set the first posts on Turkey Pond the thirteenth of June in 1941," recalls Marie Durant, who, along with Tim and two children, lived beside the mill in wooden camps. "Sized to haul on a truck bed," Tim adds. The extended Durant family, including Tim's parents and his sister's family, migrated to New Hampshire to join the timber-salvage effort. "We hauled water from a local farm," Marie Durant remembers of their sparse living conditions. Despite the hard work, the Durants were glad to have an income in post-Depression New England.

A worker rolls logs off a truck onto the ice at Turkey Pond, in Concord in February 1939. The pond received 12 million board feet of hurricane-salvaged logs. *(Photo: Bluford W. Muir, National Archives)*

Once the United States entered World War II, many businesses experienced labor shortages, as workers flocked to join the military or moved on to higher-paying jobs in support of the war effort. The Durants were no exception; they struggled to keep a crew of men working at the mill. Marie Durant spoke of the hard work and the repeated turnover of workers: "When the war hit we had trouble getting help," she recalls. "We had three crews: one working, one going, and one coming. The days were long, two shifts. A government man tallied the lumber out of the mill before it went to the sticking yard. We were paid on the tally. Most of the lumber went to a box shop in Rochester. Our record was eighteen thousand board feet in one day."

By June 1942, some 12 million board feet of logs remained floating in Turkey Pond—two and a half years after the hurricane. *(Photo courtesy of Mrs. Marie Durant)*

By June 1942, some 12 million board feet of logs remained floating in Turkey Pond—two and a half years after the hurricane. *(Photo courtesy of Mrs. Marie Durant)*

The Durant family gather around camps built along the southern shore of Turkey Pond. *(Photo courtesy of Mrs. Marie Durant)*

By the summer of 1942, it was obvious to the U.S. Forest Service program managers that the Durant family would not finish the work at Turkey Pond by the end of 1943, the program's target date. Attempts to attract other mills to the pond proved unsuccessful for the same reason—a shortage of workers. Eventually, in the fall of 1942, copying other wartime industries hiring women for what had traditionally been men's work, the U.S Forest Service constructed a sawmill designed to be operated by women. The women's sawmill was built on the north side of Turkey Pond, on land owned by St. Paul's School.

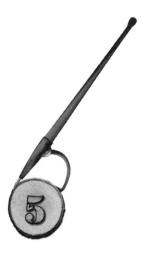

The Women's Sawmill at Turkey Pond

Construction of the second mill at Turkey Pond began in the fall of 1942, after most of the salvage effort had ended elsewhere in New England. Turkey Pond still held a huge volume of wood, and the Durants, the sawmill operating on the south shore of the pond, were losing workers to the war effort. Those remaining demanded higher wages, so the mill was in danger of defaulting on its contract with the U.S. Forest Service. To help finish sawing the remaining logs in Turkey Pond, the government decided to build a second mill on the north side of the pond rather than try to contract with a private operator. The new mill would be run by a female crew.

By 1942, the use of women as a source of labor was not unusual. More than six million women joined the workforce during World War II, many in jobs previously held by men. Women worked in shipyards, including the Portsmouth Naval Shipyard, as welders, riveters, painters,

The women's sawmill under construction at the north end of Turkey Pond.

(Photo courtesy of NH Division of Forests and Lands)

Barbara Mortensen, with her dog, Brenda, served as a fire lookout on Pine Mountain in Gorham. She also spotted planes for the Interceptor Command. Her husband, Robert Mortensen was a machinist in the Navy. *(Photo: John Collier Jr., Library of Congress, Prints & Photographs Division, FSA/OWI Collection, LC-USW3-033003-C)*

and machine operators. Women drove trucks and buses, flew planes, manufactured guns, worked on the railroads, and served in many (at the time) nontraditional jobs. The song "Rosie the Riveter" and the subsequent Norman Rockwell poster depicting Rosie eating her lunch with a riveting tool slung across her lap came to symbolize the role women played in the war effort.

Former Portsmouth, New Hampshire, mayor Eileen Foley recounts in her book, *Again, the Pleasure Is All Mine*, how she left her job as a social worker during the war to become a painter's helper at the Portsmouth Naval Shipyard. Later Eileen joined the WAC (Women's Army Corps), and was stationed at Grenier Field in Manchester. Eileen also served as a composer, or letter writer, with the awesome responsibility of writing responses to families seeking information about their loved ones.

On the home front, women also took over the running of farms and businesses. They cut firewood, tended animals, and collected scrap metal, fat, paper, and nylon. The work had to be done, and women stepped out of their traditional roles and went to work.

The sawmill at Turkey Pond was promoted as the "First in the Country" to be operated by women. U.S. Forest Service official Howard Ahlskog assured readers in an October 29, 1942, *Concord Monitor* article, "The mill will have many safety devices never before considered necessary, for the protection of the women workers. It is also being rigged up with automatically operated saws and chain drives so that there will be no heavy lifting or pulling for the feminine crew."

U.S. Forest Service manager Bob Evans described something a bit different: "We did not do anything more in setting up this mill than any employer should do if he gave full consideration to safety and working conditions for his men."

Laura Willey wrote in her scrapbook about the first days on the job: "Began work at Turkey Pond, Concord, NH, October 29, 1942. There were six of us to start on job of building the camp and helping to board up the mill."

Opposite page: The women's sawmill at Turkey Pond didn't go unnoticed. The *Concord Monitor*, the *Boston Globe*, the Associated Press, and *Life* magazine all ran stories featuring the women. (*By permission of the* Concord Monitor)

The "camp," built as a warming hut with a woodstove, would serve as the gathering place for the crew throughout the year. Rough pine milled on-site was nailed to the sides of the sawmill structure to keep out the wind, although some walls had to be left open to facilitate the logs coming into the mill and the lumber going out.

As was the Durant mill, the women's mill was oriented to the water, with a ramp that extended down into the pond. Floating logs were gathered at the ramp and hooked to a winch, which pulled up the wood into the mill.

The mill consisted of a large circular saw (the head saw); a carriage, which carried the logs through the saw; an edger, which cut off the rough edges from boards; and a trim saw, which clipped the ends. Roller decks moved the lumber throughout the mill. A blower was set up to remove sawdust from the mill.

The crew relax during a lunch break in front of the camp building. *(Photo: John Collier Jr., Library of Congress, Prints & Photographs Division, FSA/OWI Collection, LC-USW3-034123-C)*

From the U.S. Forest Service, *Washington Office Information Digest*, November 3, 1942

NETSA Sawmill to Employ Women

Because of the critical shortage in labor, NETSA is employing women to work in its sawmill at Turkey Pond, New Hampshire, on a trial basis. The sawmill is not, however, being entirely "manned" by women, as recent new dispatches indicate. Safety devices have been installed to protect the workers. Automatic saws and chain drives will eliminate much of the heavy lifting and hauling. If the venture proves a success, it is planned to employ women in other NETSA sawmills in order to complete the project within the time permitted by the contract obligations.

The finished mill on the north shore of Turkey Pond. *(Photo: John Collier Jr., Library of Congress, Prints & Photographs Division, FSA/OWI Collection, LC-USW3-034135-C)*

Clockwise from top left: Elizabeth Esty guides logs to the ramp with a pike pole. After driving a spike, which is attached to a chain, into the end of the log, Elizabeth hooks it to a winch cable. She then signals the winch operator in the mill. The winch drags logs up and into the sawmill for processing. *(Photo: John Collier Jr., Library of Congress, Prints & Photographs Division, FSA/OWI Collection LC-USW3-034103-E, 034105-E, 034100-E, and 034106-E)*

From The U. S. Forest Service, *Washington Office Information Digest*, November 19, 1942

More on Employment of Women in Sawmills

The Information Digest for November 3 mentioned the experiment being conducted by NETSA in the use of women to run a sawmill operation. Further word on this project has now been received in a note from Director Campbell, who says: The "female" mill at Turkey Pond is going along nicely. It is most surprising and gratifying to see the way those gals take hold of the job. In addition to the jobs we anticipated women could handle we have found them capable of rolling logs on the deck, running the edger, and for "show purposes" even running the head saw. Maybe it <u>will</u> be possible to actually <u>man</u> a mill 100% with women sometime in the future.

The crew assemble for a picture on January 14, 1943. Left to right: Mary Plourde, Barbara Webber, Violet Story, Carmilla Wilson, Lucy DeGreenia, Ruth DeRoche, Daisy Perkins, Laura Willey, and chimney the dog. *(Photo courtesy of John Willey)*

Women gather logs to the edge of the ramp leading up into the sawmill. *(Photo: John Collier Jr., Library of Congress, Prints & Photographs Division, FSA/OWI Collection, LC-USW3-034162-C)*

John Dunbar, age eighteen at the time, used to drive a lumber truck from the sawmill to the drying fields and thought it was funny: "Wasn't used to women doing that kind of work," he says. "That's why it stood out. Hard to believe it. Specially a lady roller [referring to the log roller Violet Story] and the whole works. There was one pretty good-sized woman and she'd take and roll the log against the head block." He described Violet Story turning the log before it passed through the saw: "When you come up on the second turn, it turns hard."

Opposite page at top: Violet Story guides a board away from head saw. The large saw in the background at left is a spare in a storage crate. *Opposite page at bottom:* Violet peels a board off a log. *(Photos: John Collier Jr., Library of Congress, Prints & Photographs Division, FSA/OWI Collection, LC-USW3-034113-C and 034046-E)*

Some women, particularly those experienced in sawmill or farm work, were hired from local families. Recruiters felt that farm and mill women would be rugged and reliable and have an understanding of the work requirements. Laura Willey and Violet Story were recruited that way. Daisy Perkins and Florence Drouin left jobs at the New Hampshire State Hospital to work at Turkey Pond, others left waitress, seamstress, and housekeeper jobs. Most were recruited through the U.S. Employment Service in Concord. The Webber sisters—Barbara, twenty-one and Norma, eighteen—came to Turkey Pond this way.

Daisy Perkins, trim saw operator (left), and Florence Drouin, pond worker (right), both left jobs at the New Hampshire State Hospital in Concord to work at Turkey Pond, where the wages were substantially higher. *(Photos: John Collier Jr., Library of Congress, Prints & Photographs Division, FSA/OWI Collection, LC-USW3-034147-C & 034095-E)*

Laura Willey, mother of four, was the head saw-filer at the mill. Her job, maintaining and sharpening the teeth of the circular saw, required considerable skill. Laura occasionally took over to spell her husband, Marshall, the sawyer, who controlled the process of making a log into lumber by guiding logs through the saw.

The job of sawyer remained a male-held position. Despite the "all-women sawmill" reputation, the government initially felt that women could not be trained as sawyers. By the end of the salvage program, that thinking had changed.

"A heavier-built woman unquestionably can be trained to saw. That is the only position that we did not train them in," said Bob Evans. Laura Willey may have been responsible for the change of heart. "My mother was very determined and, at over six feet tall, people tended to get out of her way," John Willey said.

Saw filer Laura Willey inspects the headsaw for dings, cracks, and overheating. The saw filer is one of the most highly skilled jobs in any sawmill. *(AP Photo)*

Violet Story lived on a farm in Hopkinton, a few miles to the west. The mother of six children, Violet accomplished the most physical work at the Turkey Pond sawmill—rolling logs and hefting boards. According to her son David, who was a young child at the time, his mother returned home each evening and cooked a full supper for her family. Hard work was part of her life.

Violet Story and her husband, Rapha, pose at their farm in Hopkinton. *(From Violet Story's scrapbook, courtesy of David Story)*

Violet Story enjoys a quiet moment during her lunch break. *(Photos: John Collier Jr., Library of Congress, Prints & Photographs Division, FSA/OWI Collection, LC-USW3-034031-E, 034032-E, and 034033-E)*

> ## The Photographs of John Collier Jr.
>
> John Collier Jr. (1913–1992) was born in Sparkill, New York. He was a well-known documentary photographer who worked for the federal government, specifically the FSA (Farm Security Administration) during the Depression, and later, during World War II, at the FSA, Office of War Information. The Turkey Pond images are in the Library of Congress, in the America from the Great Depression to World War II Collection: Black and White Photographs from the FSA/OWI, 1935–1945.

The starting wage for the women at Turkey Pond was four dollars per day, well above the typical women's wage at that time. It was no wonder, then, that women left the secure and warm environment of the state hospital to work out in the cold at Turkey Pond. In 1942, a female worker could expect $1.40 per day as a waitress or $1.80 as a retail clerk.

In December 1942, W. H. Drath, chief of NETSA's Production Division, wrote a letter to the director of the Wage and Hour Public Contracts Division in support of raising the women's wages to $4.50 per day once they were trained. This, he argued, would be comparable to the minimum wage paid to trained male employees. Later correspondence, in March 1943, indicated that the wages were raised.

Oliver P. Wallace (Wally), a young U.S. Forest Service log scaler, had the task of training the women recruits. In an interview in 2000, he described the women as a group of eager farm girls ready to work. Most of the training was on the job, rather than formal instruction. The women learned their jobs quickly, putting Wally out of the job within a month.

Opposite page: Ruth DeRoche, lumber stacker, was responsible for sorting and piling boards according to width, length and grade. *(Photos: John Collier Jr., Library of Congress, Prints & Photographs Division, FSA/OWI Collection, LC-USW3-034091-E, 034090-E, 034089-E, and 034088-E)*

They Sawed Up a Storm 47

"This was a cohesive group," Wally said. "I remember them as happy and hardworking. A few were local farm girls; a few like the Webber sisters were from Concord, and Laura [Willey] was used to hard work."

Barbara Webber later added this in an interview: "We were brought to work in a van from down by the state house."

Oliver P. Wallace, after serving in the military, went on to become a professor of forestry at the University of New Hampshire. "I guess I had a talent for teaching," Wally said.

The crew gathers on a summer day. Standing, left to right: Elizabeth Esty, Dorothy DeGreenia, unidentified, Violet Story, Lucy DeGreenia, Barbara Webber, Daisy Perkins. Kneeling: Norma Webber and Ruth DeRoche. *(Photo courtesy of David Story)*

Barbara Webber operated the edger and, as she said in a 2001 interview, "I knew how to make a good board. I never talked about it because if I did, no one would believe me." Barbara and her sister, Norma, then eighteen, thought it would be something interesting to do while their boyfriends were at war.

At top, Barbara Webber edges the rough sides off a pine board. During a break (below), she talks with her younger sister, Norma. *(Photos: John Collier Jr., Library of Congress, Prints & Photographs Division, FSA/OWI Collection, LC-USW3-034082-E and 034051-E)*

Barbara Webber, machine operator, was twenty-one at the time: "I did many jobs, including running the edger and the winch that brought logs up and out of the water," she said. She remembered the winter of 1943: "We wore men's boots with lots of socks to keep warm." She spoke about her experience at Turkey Pond matter-of-factly but with a great deal of pride.

Barbara Webber, at age twenty-one, was proud of her work at Turkey Pond. Now ninety, Barbara lives with her family in Maine. *(Photos: John Collier Jr., Library of Congress, Prints & Photographs Division, FSA/OWI Collection, LC-USW3-034040-E and 034042-E)*

Top left: Dorothy DeGreenia operated the winch that brought logs up out of the water into the sawmill. Top right and bottom: She spent much of her time shoveling old bark and debris out of the building. *(Photos: John Collier Jr., Library of Congress, Prints & Photographs Division, FSA/OWI Collection, LC-USW3- 034049-E, 034096-E, and 034097-E)*

The women's mill at Turkey Pond operated for a little more than a year and, despite its short life, was a success. In March 1943, R. M. Evans, assistant administrator of NETSA, Boston, was asked to comment on the effectiveness of the women's sawmill at Turkey Pond. Here is an excerpt from the National Archives:

> Non-absenteeism is one of the merits of the women's crew. The turnover was low—about 75% of the women hired at the beginning of the project stuck it out to the end. Snow, rain or subzero weather never slowed them up. They never missed a day. One woman fell in [the] pond and would not stay in the warming shack and dry off but went right on working.
>
> Briefly summarizing our women's mill crew at Turkey Pond, they were a very patriotic, loyal, high class, group of women. Too much praise cannot go down for that particular group. Newspaper publicity urged them to register with the U.S.E.S. [United States Employment Service] and all were recruited through that source. As a crew they were always on the job. They were 100% loyal to their job and proud to say they worked in a Government sawmill.

The last logs at Turkey Pond were sawn on November 23, 1943, just over five years from the date of the first log delivery to the pond.

Dorothy DeGreenia hams it up for the camera during a lunch break. Below, her sister-in-law Lucy takes a rest during lunch. Their husbands were brothers and worked as pond men, gathering logs for the sawmills at Turkey Pond. (Photos: John Collier Jr., Library of Congress, Prints & Photographs Division, FSA/OWI Collection, LC-USW3-034072-E, 034073-E, and 034074-E; below: 034149-C, 03034-E, and 03030-E)

Today, Turkey Pond is unassuming. Only a few miles from the capitol building in Concord, it is bisected by Interstate 89. Fishermen frequent an access point off Clinton Street just a few feet from where the Durant sawmill stood, and where the rowing team from St. Paul's School can be seen gliding by. Except for a historic marker on Route 13, there is little evidence of the 12 million board feet of logs dumped into the pond after the 1938 hurricane, nor of the two sawmills that were built along its shore.

One can only imagine the work of rolling logs, stacking lumber, and shoveling sawdust. The noise level would have been deafening and the strain of repetitive motion exhausting. No matter the time of year—bone-chilling cold in the winter and pitchy sawdust in the summer—the work was difficult and uncomfortable. This was not a job for the weak, but rather hard work for a group of people determined to see it through to serve their country and earn a good wage as they sawed up a storm.

Ruth DeRoche takes a nap to recover from stacking boards at the Turkey Pond sawmill. *(Photo: John Collier Jr., Library of Congress, Prints & Photographs Division, FSA/OWI Collection, LC-USW3-034028-E)*

Selected References

Allen, Everett S. *A Wind to Shake the World: The Story of the 1938 Hurricane.* Boston: Little, Brown and Company, 1976.

American Red Cross, *New York–New England Hurricane and Floods. 1938: Official Report of Relief Operations.* Washington, D.C.: The American National Red Cross, 1938.

Baker, Helen. *Women in War Industries.* Princeton, N.J.: Industrial Relations Section, Princeton University, 1942.

Barraclough, Kenneth E. *Farm Forestry in New Hampshire.* Report of Forestry and Recreation Commission, New Hampshire, 1939–40.

Berwick, Ken. Phone interview, 13 July 1998, Loudon, New Hampshire.

Burns, Cherie. *The Great Hurricane—1938.* New York: Atlantic Monthly Press, 2005.

Colby, James Sr. Interview, 3 December 1999, Boscawen, New Hampshire (notes with author).

Colman, Penny. *Rosie the Riveter: Women Working on the Home Front in World War II.* New York: Crown Publishers, 1995.

Dunbar, John. Taped interview, 9 May 2000, Henniker, New Hampshire (notes and tape with author).

Concord Daily Monitor (Concord, N.H.), 26 October 1942. "Woman-operated Sawmill First of Kind in Country, Will Start Work Soon at Turkey Pond."

Concord and Pembroke, New Hampshire Directory (1940–43, 1945), Springfield, Mass.: H. A. Manning Publishers.

Cummings, John W. *Freak Winds: New Hampshire 1938.* Manchester, N.H.: Lew A. Cummings Co., 1976.

Durant, Marie, and Tim Durant. Taped interview, 12 October 1999, Boscawen, New Hampshire (tape recording and notes with author).

Eberly, H. J. (U.S. Forest Service). *Progress in Overcoming 1938 Hurricane Disaster*, Report of the Forestry and Recreation Commission, New Hampshire: 1939–40, pp.14–16.

Federal Writers Project. *New England Hurricane: A Factual, Pictorial Record*, Boston: Hale, Cushman and Flint, 1938.

Foley, Eileen. *Again, the Pleasure Is All Mine*. Portsmouth, N.H.: Peter Randall Publisher, 2005.

Ford, Barbara Webber. Interview, 15 September 1998, Concord, New Hampshire (notes with author).

Gudmundsson, B. J., Doug Chadwick. *Out of the Storm: The Galford Lumber Company Documentary Project*, Lewisburg, WVa. Patchwork Films, 2001. http://www.patchworkfilms.com/galford/

Jones, Janet. "Lumberjills Replace Lumberjacks." *Boston Sunday Globe*, 20 December 1942.

McCarthy, Joe. *Hurricane*. New York: American Heritage Press, 1969.

Minsinger, William Elliott, M.D. *The 1938 Hurricane: An Historical and Pictorial Summary*. Milton, Mass: Blue Hills Observatory, 1988.

New England Forest Emergency Project and Northeast Timber Salvage Administration, 1938 to 1943 (various correspondence, photos, contracts, and reports), U.S. Department of Agriculture, Forest Service, Entry 19, Record Group 95. The National Archives and Records Administration, Waltham, Mass.

New England Hurricane, Federal Writers Project of the Works Progress Administration. Boston: Hale, Cushman & Flint, 1938.

New Hampshire Forest Market Report, University of New Hampshire Extension Service, Bulletin no. 61, November 1941, K. E. Barraclough, Extension forester.

New Hampshire Forest Market Report, University of New Hampshire Extension Service, winter 1938–39, Extension Circular 219. Durham, N.H.: December 1938.

Page, Ralph. Account of the 1938 hurricane, *Newsletter of the Historical Society of Cheshire County, New Hampshire*. September 1988. Special Collections, Dimond Library, University of New Hampshire.

Perspectives on the Employment Service. Washington, D.C.: National League of Cities and U.S. Conference of Mayors, 1973.

Report of Forestry and Recreation Commission, New Hampshire, 1937–38, pp. 56–58.

Report of the U.S. Forest Service Programs Resulting from the New England Hurricane of September 21, 1938. Boston: Northeastern Timber Salvage Administration, February 1943.

Richards, Tudor. Interview and field visit, November 1998, Turkey Pond, Concord, New Hampshire.

Scotti, R. A. *Sudden Sea: The Great Hurricane of 1938.* Boston: Little, Brown & Company, 2003.

Wallace, Oliver P. Taped interview, 29 October 2000. New London, New Hampshire (tape and notes with author).

Willey, Glenn. Interview at grave site of Laura and Marshall Willey, Loudon, New Hampshire (notes with author).

Willey, John. Various interviews. Andover, New Hampshire (notes with author).

Other Resources

Brokaw, Tom. *The Greatest Generation.* New York: Random House, 1998.

Duchesne, Helen L. *In Their Time.* Bristol, N.H.: Bear Mountain Cove Press, 1997.

Hartmann, Susan M. *The Homefront and Beyond: American Women in the 1940s.* Boston: G. K. Hall & Co., 1982.

Frank, Miriam, Marilyn Ziebarth, and Connie Field. "Rosie the Riveter." *Society* (March/April 1984): 75–80.

Gluck, Sherna Berger. *Rosie the Riveter Revisited.* Boston: Twayne Publishers, 1987.

Harris, Mark Jonathan, Franklin D. Mitchell, and Steven J. Schechter. "Rosie the Riveter Remembers." *American Heritage* (February/March 1984): 94–103.

Honey, Maureen. *Creating Rosie the Riveter.* Amherst: The University of Massachusetts Press, 1984.

Kennedy, Susan Estabrook. *America's White Working-Class Women: A Historical Bibliography.* New York: Garland Publishing, 1981.

Kerber, Linda K., and Sherron Lane De Hart. *Women's America: Refocusing the Past.* New York: Oxford University Press, 1995.

Koop, Allen V. *Stark Decency: German Prisoners of War in a New England Village.* Hanover, N.H.: University Press of New England, 1988.

Milkman, Ruth. *Gender at Work.* Urbana and Chicago: University of Illinois Press, 1987.

Nichols, Nancy A. "What Ever Happened to Rosie the Riveter?" *Harvard Business Review*, July/August 1993.

Weatherford, Doris. *American Women and World War II.* New York: Facts on File, 1990.

Wessels, Tom. *Reading the Forested Landscape: A Natural History of New England.* Woodstock, Vt: The Countryman Press, 1997.

Yellen, Emily. *Our Mothers' War: American Women at Home and at the Front during World War II.* New York: Free Press, 2004.

About the Author

Sarah Shea Smith is Extension professor and specialist, Forest Industry, at the University of New Hampshire Cooperative Extension, a post she's held since 1989. Sarah has worked as a hardwood lumber inspector, a teacher, and a door-and-trim carpenter. She holds a bachelor of science degree in forestry and a master's in occupational education from the University of New Hampshire. Sarah and her husband, Peter, live in Newmarket, New Hampshire.

Index

Again, The Pleasure is All Mine (Foley), 34
Ahlskog, Howard, 35
Alegrete, S.S. (cargo ship), 5
Andover, New Hampshire, viii
Atlantic City, New Jersey, 6*m*,7

Bigelow, Hayes, 20
Blue Hill Observatory, 9
Boscawen, New Hampshire, 16, 17, 21
Burlington, Vermont, 8

Campbell, Director, 39
Cape Hatteras, North Carolina, 5, 6*m*
Carinthia (liner), 6
CCC. *See* Civilian Conservation Corps
Chadwick, Doug, 21
Chesterfield, New Hampshire, 22*p*
Civilian Conservation Corps (CCC), 13
Clinton Street (Concord, New Hampshire), 54
Colby, Jim, Sr., 21
College Woods, 1
Collier, John, Jr., viii*p*, ix*p*, 34, 36, 37, 38, 40, 41, 42, 45, 46, 47, 49, 50, 51, 52, 53
Concord Monitor (newspaper), 35, 35*p*
Concord, New Hampshire, viii, 9*p*, 11*p*, 21, 25–29, 26*p*, 27*p*, 28*p*, 42, 54. *See also* Turkey Pond
Connecticut, 6*m*, 7, 8, 14*c*
Cummings Printing, 2, 3, 8, 9, 10

DeGreenia, Dorothy, 48*p*, 51*p*, 53*p*
DeGreenia, Lucy, 39*p*, 48*p*, 53*p*
DeRoche, Ruth, 39*p*, 47*p*, 48*p*, 54*p*
Drath, W.H., 46
Drouin, Florence, 42, 42*p*

Dunbar, John, 17, 40
Durant, H.S., 25–26, 29, 29p, 31
Durant, Marie, 25, 26, 27, 28, 29, 29p
Durant, Tim, 25

Eastern Pine Sales Corporation, 24
Employment Service, U.S., 42, 52
Esty, Elizabeth, 38p, 48p
Evans, Bob, 35, 43
Evans, R.M., 52

Farm Security Administration (FSA), 46
First Congregational Church, 10p
Foley, Eileen, 34
Forest Notes, 15
Forest Service, U.S., ix, 13, 15–17, 15p, 19, 19p, 20p, 21, 26, 29, 31, 35, 37, 39
forests, 10, 11. *See also* timber salvage operations
Forests and Lands, N.H. Division of, 33
Freak Winds (Cummings Printing), 2, 3, 8, 9, 10

Galford, Glen, 21
Galford Lumber Company, 20p, 21
Gilford, New Hampshire, 16p, 18p
Gorham, New Hampshire, 34p
Grantham, New Hampshire, 15p
Green Bank, West Virginia, 20, 21
Grenier Field (Manchester, New Hampshire), 34
Gudmundsson, B.J., 21

Hartford, Connecticut, 7
Hopkinton, New Hampshire, 44p
hurricane, ix, 1–3, 2p, 3p, 5–11, 6m, 8p, 9p, 10p, 11p, 54. *See also* timber salvage operations

Kaylor, Joseph, 15p
Keene, New Hampshire, 10p

Lee, Helen Joy, 7
Leighton, Roger, 1
Lily Pond, 16p
L.L. Bean, iip
log branding, 19, 20p
log prices, 19, 21, 24
Long Island, New York, 7, 8, 9, 10
lumber, 23p, 24, 47p

Manchester, New Hampshire, 3p, 34
Massachusetts, 6m, 8, 9, 10, 14c
Mechanic Street, 10p
Minsinger, William Elliott, 7, 8
Mortenson, Barbara, 34p
Mortenson, Robert, 34p
Mount Washington (New Hampshire), 9
Muir, Bluford W., 15, 18, 20, 22, 26

Narragansett Bay, 7
Nashua, New Hampshire, 2p
Natti, Ted, 15
NETSA. *See* Northeast Timber Salvage Administration
New England State Foresters, 13
New England Timber, 21
New Hampshire, 14c, 15, 24. *See also* names of individual cities and towns
New Hampshire State Hospital, 42, 46
New Haven, Connecticut, 8
The 1938 Hurricane (Minsinger), 7, 8. *See also* hurricane
Northeast Timber Salvage Administration (NETSA), 16–17, 19, 21, 24, 37, 39, 46, 52
Northeast Timber Salvage Program, ix
The Northern Logger (magazine), vii
Northern Woodlands (magazine), vii
Northfield, Massachusetts, 20p

Old Lowell Road, 2p

Out of the Storm: the Galford Lumber Company Documentary Project (Gadmundsson), 21

Page, Ralph, 1–2
Pearl Harbor, 24
Perkins, Daisy, 39*p*, 42, 42*p*, 48*p*
Peterborough, New Hampshire, 7, 8*p*
Pine Mountain (Gorham, New Hampshire), 34*p*
Plourde, Mary, 39*p*
Portsmouth Naval Shipyard, 31, 34
property loss, 2, 3*p*, 7-8, 8*p*, 9, 9*p*, 10, 10*p*, 11*p*
Providence, Rhode Island, 7

Rhode Island, 6*m*, 7, 14*c*
Rockwell, Norman, 34
Rollins Park (Concord, New Hampshire), 11*p*, 21
Roosevelt, Franklin D., 15
Rosie the Riveter, 34

Saint Paul's School, 29, 54
Sargent Garage, 10*p*
saw-filer, 42, 43*p*
sawing rates, 19, 21, 24
sawmills
  timber salvage operation and, 21, 22*p*, 24
  Turkey Pond, ix, 25–29, 26*p*, 27*p*, 28*p*, 31–54, 32*p*, 34*p*, 35*p*, 36*p*, 38*p*, 39*p*, 40*p*, 41*p*, 42*p*, 43*p*, 44*p*, 45*p*, 47*p*, 48*p*
  women working in, 29, 31–54, 32*p*, 34*p*, 35*p*, 36*p*, 38*p*, 39*p*, 40*p*, 41*p*, 42*p*, 43*p*, 44*p*, 45*p*, 47*p*, 48*p*
sawyer, 22*p*, 42–43
scaler, 19, 19*p*, 20*p*, 46
Scotti, R.A., 7
Silbulkin Shoe Company, 3*p*
Silver, Sam, 16
Sobel, Mildred, ii*p*
Society for the Protection of New Hampshire Forests, 14–15
Story, David, 44, 48

Story, Rapha, 44*p*
Story, Violet, viii*p*, 39p, 40, 41p, 42, 44, 44*p*, 45*p*, 48*p*
Sudden Sea (Scotti), 7

timber salvage operations, 13–24, 14*c*, 15*p*, 16*p*, 17*p*, 18*p*, 19*p*, 20*p*, 21*p*, 22*p*, 23*p*. *See also* sawmills
timber volumes, 13-14
Turkey Pond (Concord, New Hampshire), viii, ix, 25–29, 26*p*, 27*p*, 28*p*, 31–54, 32*p*, 34*p*, 35*p*, 36*p*, 38*p*, 39*p*, 40*p*, 41*p*, 42*p*, 43*p*, 44*p*, 45*p*, 47*p*, 48*p*

University of New Hampshire, 1
University of New Hampshire Cooperative Extension, 17, 18, 19, 22, 23

Vermont, 6*m*, 8, 14*c*

WAC. *See* Women's Army Corp
wages, 42, 46
Wallace, Oliver P., 46, 48
warming hut, 36, 36*p*
Washington Office Information Digest (Forest Service, U.S.), 37, 39
Weather Bureau, U.S., 5, 7
Webber, Barbara, ii*p*, viii*p*, 39*p*, 42, 48, 48*p*, 49, 49*p*, 50, 50*p*
Webber, Norma, ii*p*, 42, 48, 48*p*, 49, 49*p*
West Virginia, 21
White Mountains, 10
Wilkens Sawmill, 22*p*
Willey, John, viii–ix, 39, 43
Willey, Laura, ix, 35, 39*p*, 42, 43, 43*p*, 48
Willey, Marshall, 42
Williams, Frank, 21
Wilson, Carmilla, 39*p*
women
    sawmill work and, 29, 31–54, 32*p*, 34*p*, 35*p*, 36*p*, 38*p*, 39*p*, 40*p*, 41*p*, 42*p*, 43*p*, 44*p*, 45*p*, 47*p*, 48*p*
    in World War II, ix, 24, 26, 31, 34

Women's Army Corp (WAC), 34
Works Progress Administration (WPA), 13
World War II, ix, 24, 26, 31, 34
WPA. *See* Works Progress Administration